Momentum Trading

Trading In Stock Market

By: Priyank Gala

Published By:

Priyank Gala

©Copyright 2015 –: Priyank Gala

ISBN-13: 978-1517565718
ISBN-10: 1517565715

Table of Contents

Chapter 1: All about Momentum Trading

People often confuse Momentum Trading with the concepts of trend trading, and also with the concepts of swing trading.

A trader involved with trend trading wants to earn profits by keeping track of trending stocks, that stays in trend for at least a few days, a few weeks or even a few months.

A trader involved in swing trading keeps a track of the changes in trend of stocks, mainly the short term reversals that is constant only for a few days.

A trader involved in momentum trading is bound by the limits of time, and usually will open and close a certain trading position in one single trading day, which limits his or her options of conducting the trade to the opening and closing hours of the stock market.

In a much simpler and easily understandable way, a momentum trader is always on the lookout for stocks with rapidly moving prices on high volume. The momentum trader will buy the stock if the price of the stock moves up, and will initiate a short position if the stock price moves down. Some factors that tingle the interest of all momentum traders are:

- Price move
- Volatility
- Trading volume

Owing to the fact the momentum trading depends on these three above mentioned factors, we can quite easily judge the time limitation of momentum traders. We can also judge the variety of stocks which might interest a momentum trader.

Chapter 2: How to become a Momentum Trader?

People often think that traders are born with the inherent skill of trading like an expert, but this is not true. All momentum traders have to go through rigorous training to reach the position of an expert trader. Traders have to invest a lot of discipline and dedication to reach the point of success in the field of momentum trading.

Chapter 3: Risks involved with momentum trading

Apart from the wrong decisions made by the traders, there are certain other risks associated with momentum trading that every trader must go through. These risks affect mostly those traders who are new in the field of momentum trading. If a trader realises the existence of such risks, and understands how to handle or tackle them, he or she will be able to avoid all such risks and boost the profit margin as well as their level of experience.

Closing on a trade before time

It is always advisable to wait and watch before closing a trade. Any trader must wait and see the development rate of an already initiated momentum trade and then close on it. Over-eagerness leads to heavy losses.

Delayed exit from the trade

Initial saturation signals may not be able to indicate the end point of any momentum trade, but even so, waiting for an indefinite period may be very harmful for a particular trader dealing in momentum trading. It is always advisable that you forego a few extra profit dollars than loose every single dime by waiting too long. If the momentum of the stock changes, then it won't be long before the trader incurs a heavy loss, because expert traders will know what to do when the momentum is altered.

Low levels of focus and concentration

All momentum traders must dedicate their complete concentration on all their trades. If there is any lack of concentration, traders might quite easily miss certain surprise moves occurring in the stock market.

Failure to quickly cut losses

Amateur traders will often make the mistake of believing that an already breached price level may be achieved once again and end up losing a lot of money while the stock goes down. These traders need to close out on a trade much earlier in such cases.

Going against all momentum trading ethics and holding on to a stock for more than one day

No momentum trader should ever hold on to a stock for more than one day. If any stock is held overnight, then it goes beyond all the concepts of momentum trading, and accordingly, they will be held solely responsible if the stock price goes south.

Chapter 4: Proper selection of stocks for momentum trading

Long term trends do not matter to any momentum trends, nor do any sort of company or business fundamentals. You will not find a single momentum trader who will be worried about the future numbers of any particular industrial sector or company. But they will always be interested about stocks which are being or have been highlighted in any financial news bulletin. Any sort of financial news is always interesting for any momentum trader.

Any kind of news, be it breaking or financial, will have a certain affect on stock prices. But, a trader dealing in momentum trading will keep one thing in mind – this affect may take the stock price either up or down - there is no fixed trend. For instance, a company may earn a lot of profit, but its stock prices may still go down and cause heavy losses for all traders. Similarly, a deal not going through for any company may in turn increase the stock price.

In short, it is wise not to be dependent on news bulletins while choosing stock for momentum trading. Try to go with the concepts of short term volatility in stock prices.

Chapter 5: Optimum time for trading

Let us talk about finding the most optimum time to look for opportunities related to momentum trading.

The best way to identify the most opportune time is to keep a lookout for financial news such as price sensitive announcements and / or company results. Almost all companies release such financial and business news announcements when the stock market closes for the day, so that they can avoid the problem of insider dealing and premature leak of confidential information.

The volatility of share prices normally increases on the anticipation of any sort of announcement or at the end of a trading day. Almost the entirety of the last hour volatile trend is caused by traders dealing with momentum trading as they open and closes on short term stock positions.

Once any company releases any sort of news right before the stock market opens, investors will be understand the meaning of the announcement and facilitate all their trades in an according manner. Investors, who hold discretional accounts, usually monitor their brokers while they are buying or selling stock for them, because the reactions of all brokers depend on the changing trends in the market.

This form of "reactionary" trade usually takes place within the first hour of a trading day.

Momentum trading in single stocks is considered to be the most common factor of the entire stock market. But momentum traders may be in search of opportunities for momentum trading in various other markets. Geopolitical events, war, release of economic data and natural catastrophes may be primary factors that affect the entire stock market scenario.

Chapter 6: Why volume is important?

Any stock may start to move up or down once a company has released any sort of important announcement. And you will notice that a momentum trader will be the very first person who aims at benefiting from said movement. The trader will wait for the establishment of the stock's short term trend, and would also anticipate the establishment of alteration in price and trend with respect to high share trading volumes.

Stocks with low volume movement usually don't live to tell the tale, and lose their momentum as traders step in to the share market. These very traders also step into the market when the trading volume of stocks is quite high. The basic concept in this case is a simple psychology – buyers who buy large volumes of stocks will inspire other buyers to do the same.

This very concept differentiates normal traders from momentum traders, because these momentum traders are always on the lookout for trading volume of a short term nature, and profit from such short term trends. Many other traders, e.g. swing traders, also keep the changing volume and trend in mind, but momentum traders hold change in volume as a confirmation to directional velocity of a short term nature.

So, what have we learnt? Let's take a small recap:

- The trading facilitated by momentum traders will be based completely on volatility, and the choice to wait for opportunities brought forward by company news and announcements.

- They are always on the lookout for stocks that move only in one direction, with the volume, trend and number of traders proving the popular concept of directional impetus.

- They will let others go for a stock, and wait for the right moment when the stock gains proper momentum.

Chapter 7: Formulating proper covered calls

After selecting the particular stocks that offer good returns on investment, the following step is to purchase the stock position. You can always go for brokers like TD Ameritrade for this very purpose. Check out the link given below:

https://www.scottrade.com/

You need to ensure that you have proper authorization for trading in call options along with other stocks in your brokerage account with any firm you choose.

In this method of stock trading, which I am trying to describe, you will first have to buy a certain stock. Then you will have to sell a particular "covered call" against the very stock which you purchased, which is sometimes known as "writing covered calls". The very word "covered" refers to the call which you sell on any market gets the support of the one single true fact that you are the owner of a certain permissible number of shares of any underlying stock, so that you may satisfy the requirements pertaining to the contract of call options, if the contract is "called" by the person who owns the call. If the call sold by you is exercised properly, the broker you have hired will sell your stock automatically provided it is covered by the call sold by you, to the person who owns the call.

The main objective that you need to follow is that you must sell your call options so that you can accomplish the following things:

1. You will get immediate cash into your account by selling covered call options. Let us take a look at an example. If you sell a total of 5 call "contracts", which is equal to almost 500 shares, and the quoted price per share was USD 2.00, then USD 1000.00 will be credited to your account right after your order to sell the option is processed on the trade of a certain options exchange.

2. You usually sell a certain call option that is about to expire in a month's time, and sometimes you repeat this process on probably the same stock, in case it is not called. If, in any case, the stock is called, you can

re-purchase it almost immediately and similarly sell a certain new call on the stock, if you get an acceptable price.

Or you have the option of investing the money you have earned from any called stock in a different investment option which can provide a fine opportunity to sell all the other contracts of covered calls.

When a certain stock is "called", it will be sold automatically out of your trading account on your behalf by the brokerage firm you have hired at a target price of the option contract sold by you.

For this very reason, you should remember that you must sell only those sell option contracts that are profitable even after the stock is called, offering a much higher amount of profit once the called option is sold. These options are usually known as "out of the money options", as the target achievable price of a particular option is much higher the actual price of the stock at the time of quoting the option.

You also have the option of selling "at the money" options if you are anticipating any decrease in stock prices and accumulated value or you want to remove a particular stock from your trading portfolio.

A certain "at the money" stock option is the option where the quoted strike or target price is almost similar to the stock price as it was during filing the quotation.

Again, from the point of view of selling options, you will also be able to sell something that is known as "in the money" options. These options usually refer to the concept that the current quoted stock price is much higher than the quoted strike price. If you sell an "in the money" option, the stock will be called from you at a much lower price.

3. If you sell a certain covered call on a stock, you can provide some downward protection on the stock for yourself. For instance, if you plan to sell a certain covered call that gives you 8% cash as measured against the total cost of purchasing a certain stock, and the stock goes down by almost 7%, you will still have a profit margin or be in a healthy break even position. You should always keep the commission factor in mind when you are calculating the yields of your option, and also keep

another fact in mind, that there is also the matter of a commission if any of your stocks are "called" by the particular owner of that particular option.

In case of American options, these can be called at any time before it expires, so you must constantly keep on checking your trading account on a daily basis and keep your eyes open for anything like this. But the case is not so in case of European options, which can be called only after expiration.

In normal scenarios, options are usually not exercised until after they are expired. By the time the options expire, some other individual might own the option sold by you, who may or may not be the original buyer, who purchased the option. It is not a matter of concern for you. Several call options go through the process of buying and selling even before it expires.

"At the money" and / or "in the money" stock options are usually not sold until certain conditions are fulfilled. These conditions are given below:

A. The price of the option earns a profit when sold
B. The value of the stock declines in accordance with the market scenario or some other factors that may affect the price of stock

We often plan on removing certain stock options from our profitable portfolio. But you can still receive a premium for the purpose of improving the total cash received by you from eliminating a certain stock if you allow it to be called from your trading account, while still enjoying the benefits of receiving cash from the sale of the option, along with the cash received from the call of the stock. In such a case, you don't have to for an outright sale.

If there is any downward slope in the price of the stock, and you still have not exercised the option, you can still continue the procedure of selling certain options on the stock following the "at the money" or "in the money" trends, until the option is successfully sold. This will help you to increase your cash flow, and earn a healthy profit with time.

Keep one thing in mind, the stock option you just sold may increase in value before its actual expiration time, thereby showing itself as an incurred loss in your trading account. Don't waste your time in trying to buy back that stock option. This could mean a huge loss for you in monetary terms. Always remember that this increased value is caused by the increase in price of all your underlying stock options.

If your underlying stock goes up in value while the stock option remains active, the option itself will increase in value as well. The case is similar if the underlying stock decreases in value.

For example, the price of the option may decline by as less as USD 0.03 on every share. If this decrease takes place, you can buy the option back by "buying to close". You will be able to sell a brand new stock option for the following month if you think it to be reasonable.

Whatever the case may be, the option will expire sooner or later, and it may either expire in a worthless position, or someone will call the option at even a penny more that the actual strike price.

When the option expires in a worthless position, you will earn a hundred percent profit when you sell the call option, and you will have earned a healthy income by exercising the option contract.

If a small decline in stock value does not bother you, you do have the option of selling a brand new call option in the upcoming month on the same stock. If you can choose the most suitable option so as to keep the option strike value well within limits, you will be able to sell options repeatedly on the very same stock, and earn a significant amount of long term profit.

Let us now look at an example. You are buying 600 shares of a certain stock at USD 40.00 per share (a USD 24,000.00 investment) and you sell the USD 45.00 strike May 2015 option for the bidding price of USD 1.80 per share, USD 1,080.00 cash is credited to your account.

Make a note of this – when you sell or write an option, you may probably get the "bid" price. If you buy the option you will probably be paying the "ask" price. On certain stocks with a low volume, the spread between the ask and bid prices can be very large.

Fig. 3, showcases the "option chain" for 19th May, 2015 expiration stock options. This chain is actually the one found on the very next day from the quoted option of USD 1.80, and you will see that the bid option for USD 45.00

strike value has dropped to USD 0.80, due to a downward fluctuation of your underlying stock price.

So you need to be aware that all option prices may change without a moment's notice, and if a good price for an option catches your attention in case of a particular trading day, you should definitely "strike the iron while it's still hot" because the price may drop even lower the following day. You also need to take special care because options prices might decay with time due to stagnancy of the stock price.

Checkout the appendix to get a lesson on basic primer, along with a few vital tips

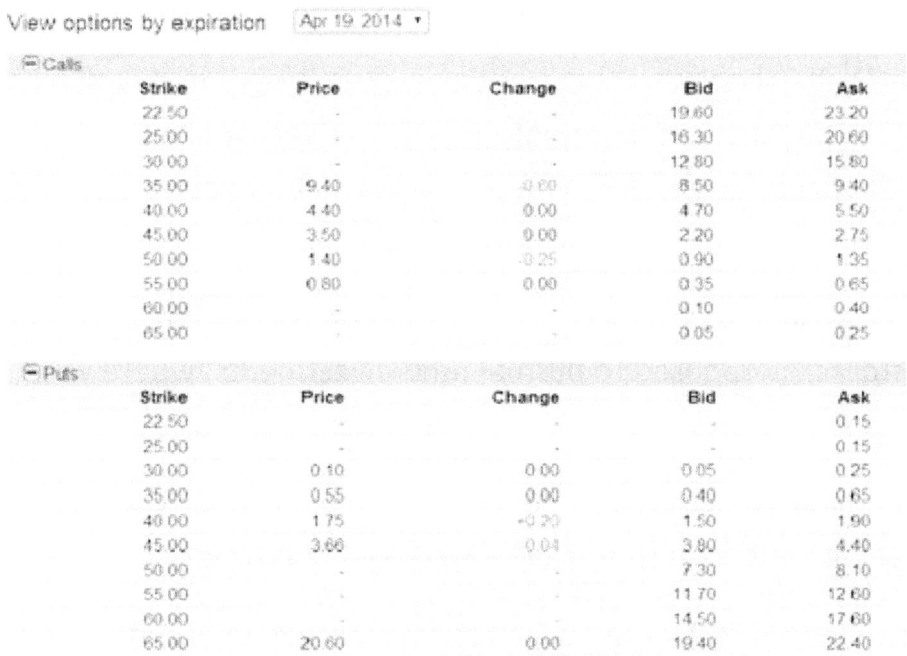

Fig Google Finance's Typical Option "Chain"

Let's look at a hypothetical scenario. The price of a certain stock never goes above USD 45.00 during a single month, so you have earned USD 1,080.00 on your investment, before commissions of 3.47% for a particular month which is equal to just over 41% every year, if you can reach this target almost every month.

Now let us suppose that a certain stock goes up to USD 46.00 before the option expires, and your stock of 600 shares is called at the strike price of USD 45.00.

So now your stock option is sold for USD 27,000.00 and you will still have USD 1,080.00 for the covered call option sold by you on the stock. Your total profit amount is

USD 27,000 + USD 1,080 – USD 24,000 = USD 4,080

and the percentage of your profit is

100 * ((USD 4080 / USD 24000) -1) = 21.7%

This figure is quite impressive for a single month.

You can now see quite clearly see the profit advantage associated with purchasing momentum stocks that rapidly increase in price and allow you to exercise the high priced "out of the money" options so that you can add it to your profit margin.

But be aware of the high risks associated with momentum trading or trading in any individual stocks, as opposed to mutual fund investments, where your investment will really be secure and in a risk free environment.

Also, care must be taken in case of mutual funds investments as well, because some funds develop very slowly and have an extremely slow growth rate.

So if you plan to invest in certain individual stocks through momentum trading, or through any other trading strategy, you should keep a check on your investment amount and properly diversify all your stock holdings as per the assets available to you.

Chapter 8: Strategy used for momentum trading

Momentum trading is all about strong focus and discipline while executing a certain trading strategy. Though momentum traders only trade for short periods, they spend a lot of time by analysing the potential of any trade before they open a certain position. In short, decisions for trading can be made within just a few minutes after a stock market opens for a day. A five step process if followed for this.

Step 1: Selecting the right stocks

A momentum trader's trading hours are more than an hour more than any other trader's trading day. They will search the internet for latest news that may affect the stock market. These traders usually use stock screening monitors and charts so as to get alerts regarding the stocks that have changed position due to any news release. Latest forecasts from expert analysts are also helpful to these traders.

Many of these traders dealing with momentum trading usually make it a point to analyse trades made in any after-market scenario. This can help them understand the movement of stocks on the very next day, and only after understanding the scenario can they make trading decisions.

Most experienced traders normally analyse open interest in call and try to put options so that others may have an increased interest in buying and selling stocks.

After listing the most potential stocks, the trader will shortlist his or her own preferred stocks on his or her trading platform right before the day's trading begins.

Step 2: The open market

After the market opens, the momentum trader will track his shortlisted stocks and their individual performance. The built up expectations of the trader, formed by a pre market analysis, will help to understand the stock's movement. The best moving stocks are easy and profitable targets for the trader.

After establishing a certain price movement, the trader will take a look at a two vital elements:

Volume – If the price move was not affected by significant volume, the trader will remove the stock from his or her shortlist. Significant volume differs for each stock – this is a known fact. A big cap stock usually trades with a larger volume, while a mid cap stock deals with lower volume.

Level 2 interest – The level 2 monitoring screen is all about informing the traders about buying and selling interest at a certain price. Let us look at a Level 2 page example and see what it contains:

- The Bid price
- The code of the firm on the bid
- The number of shares people have bid for at a certain price (x100)

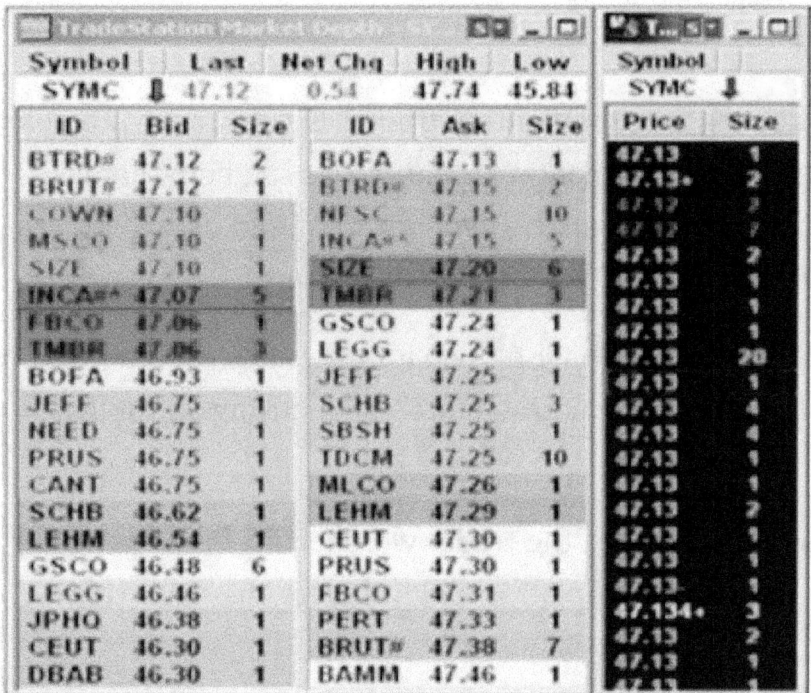

From such a level 2 screen, a trader dealing momentum stocks will assess the bid's strength and ask accordingly. This will also assist them in ascertaining potential levels of trading. This page acts as a dynamic indicator, with continuous entrance of buying and selling interests in the market.

Step 3: Information received by the trader from the chart

Any momentum trader will refer to the stock chart. Breaking of support levels or reference levels will be a very useful reference for all traders. If these levels are broken with the aid of momentum and are supported by adequate volume, the trader can quite easily open a stock position.

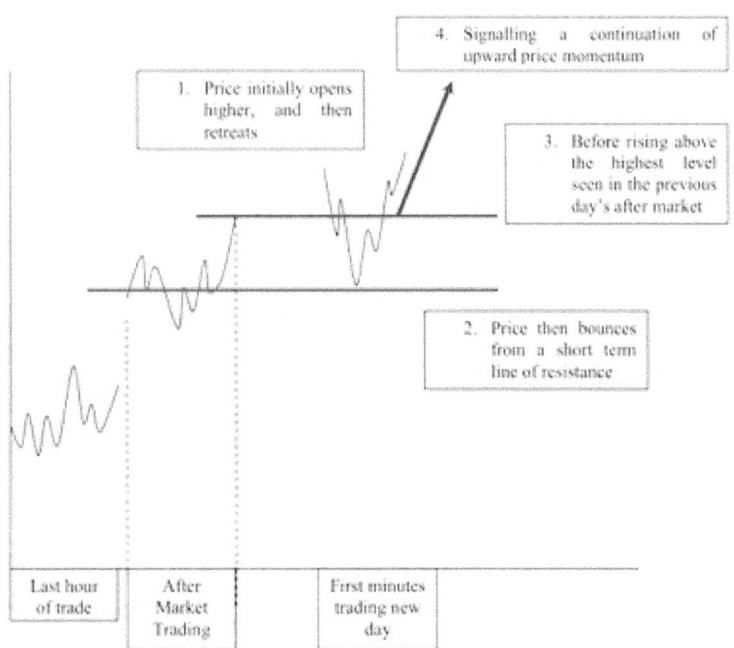

Another factor that a momentum trader may look into is the comparison of the previous day's after-market trading figures to the opening trading figures. The diagram given below showcases a sample trading decision working in continuance with the movement of stock prices as expected by any expert momentum trader.

If the original price has not been recovered from the pull back scenario within a few minutes of the opening bell, and continued to sloop down on a downward trend, going even lower than the after-market high figures, an expert momentum trader will never open a long term stock position.

Step 4- Screening and selection of stocks with high momentum

The very first thing is shortlist high momentum stocks based on real factual data. Some criteria that could help you to choose such high momentum stocks are really easy to adhere to. Read the criteria mentioned below to get detailed info:

1. The stock price falls below USD 50.00, or a certain price that lets you purchase up to 100 shares of each stock, that could help you build a diversified and profitable portfolio.
2. Keep an eye out for stocks that are at least priced USD 10.00 so that traders can get a better selection of options on a good quality high momentum stock.
3. Stocks that have gone up by at least 150% in the last one year are a good choice for professional traders.
4. Stocks that trade in at least 150000 shares on a daily basis are active stocks and are good for trading.
5. Keep a look out for stocks that have a fixed price to earnings ratio of a minimum of 3, but less than the maximum limit of 120. These stocks are quite profitable, and are high momentum trading favourites.
6. Stocks with a total market cap of almost USD 1 billion or higher is a perfect stock that fulfils the criteria.

Keep one thing in mind – sticking to the criteria as if they were words from the Bible would be a big mistake, because you may end up with an empty portfolio.

Keeping all the above mentioned points in mind, the table given below shows what happens when the above criteria can be profitably used with the help of the Google stock screener made available through Google Finance. Follow the link given below:

https://www.google.com/finance?ei=QciEXU-iiJC.unsOesaOE#stockscreener

In the actual screen results as shown in Fig. 1 below, we have made use of an actual criteria as given below:

Market cap USD 970 Million to USD 980 Million PE 3.54 to 120

52 week change in price 139 minimum last price USD 10.23 to USD 53

Fig. 8.1 showcases a standard Google setup for the screener. In certain cases, you may not be able to set the exact values as per your preference with the given "slider" system of entering data, but there still is the advantage that you will be able to see the proper distribution of certain values in certain particular categories of the screener. So you set certain limit points with the help of this distribution.

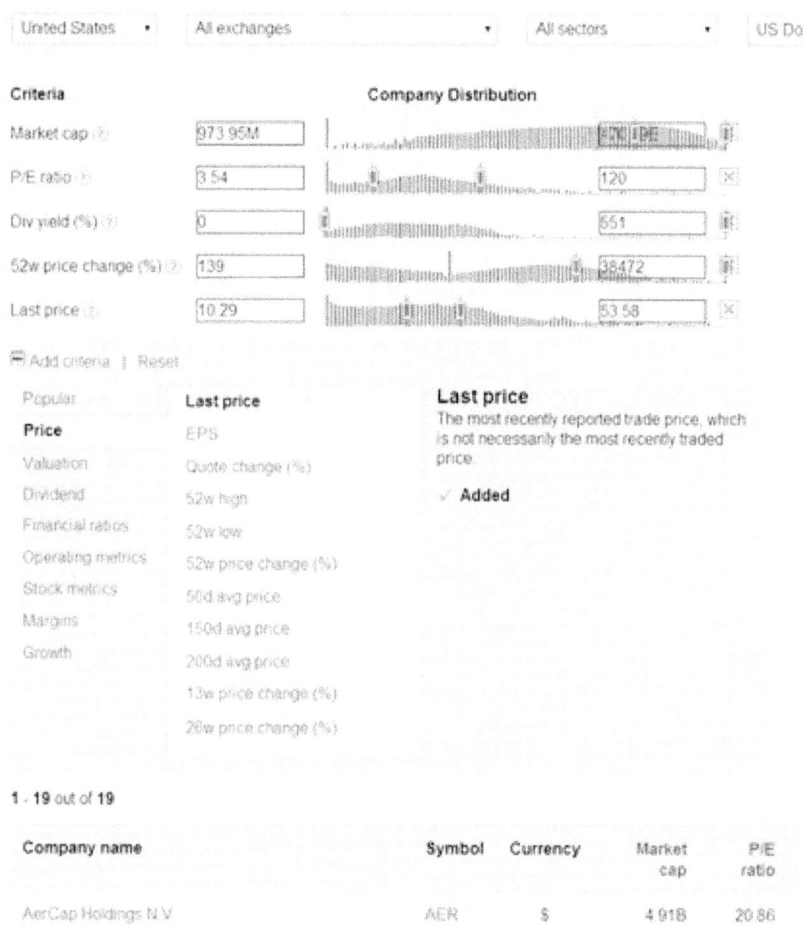

Fig. 8.2 High Momentum Stocks' preliminary screen (Data as on the 3rd of May, 2014)

You will see in Fig. 1 that there exists a large variation in PE, price, 52 week price change and market cap. Some stocks even pay off dividends to the share holders. You should remember that only 18 out of all the stocks checked by Google met the criteria of being high momentum stocks, so the choice becomes quite easy.

But any further study and screening will definitely shorten the list of selective stocks.

You can check Fig 8.2 to understand the tabulated form of the research of the stocks as per the information displayed by an initial data screen. You will see certain listed stocks that have been rated as "no buy" for any expert trader's momentum trading portfolio, simply based on some uncovered facts found during the research.

For instance, in Fig 8.2 for TAL Education (XRS), we have given the "no buy" rating, but the dividend paid by the stock may interest several buyers. The stock is not suitable as per other criteria used for picking high momentum stocks.

It is also a true fact that the various other stocks mentioned in Fig. 2 are listed as "no buy" stocks. But it does not necessarily mean that these are underperforming stocks. In all actuality, these stocks may be perfect for long term investments.

Company name	Symbol	Last price	April 2014 Call	Option Price	% Option	Chart	Profit news	Buy?
AerCap Holdings N.V.	AER	42.35	42.5	1.95	4.60	good	good	yes
Bitauto Hldg Ltd (ADR)	BITA	42.9	45	3.2	7.46	good	good	yes
CalAmp Corp.	CAMP	34.28	35	1.8	5.25	good	ok	yes
Ctrip.com International, Ltd. (ADR)	CTRP	53.54	55	3.3	6.16	good	good	yes
E-House (China) Holdings Limited (ADR)	EJ	14.65	15	1.15	7.85	good	ok	yes
Federal-Mogul Corp	FDML	19.34	20	0.65	3.36	poor	slim	no
Himax Technologies, Inc. (ADR)	HIMX	14.42	15	0.95	6.59	good	good	yes
Lannett Company, Inc.	LCI	45.6	50	1.6	3.51	good	v. goo	yes
Methode Electronics Inc.	MEI	34.9	35	2.7	7.74	good	good	yes
Micron Technology, Inc.	MU	24.75	25	1.59	6.42	good	good	yes
Navios Maritime Holdings Inc.	NM	11.48	12.5	0.35	3.05	poor	fair	no
Nexstar Broadcasting Group, Inc.	NXST	41.99	45	1.1	2.62	poor	bad	no
Phoenix New Media Ltd ADR	FENG	12.71	15	0.4	3.15	poor	ok	no
Santarus, Inc.	SNTS	31.96	NA	NA		ok	ok	no
SunPower Corporation	SPWR	35.43	36	2.29	6.46	ok	slim	no
TAL Education Group (ADR)	XRS	23.94	25	0.7	2.92	ok	good	no
TASER International, Inc.	TASR	19.63	20	1.05	5.35	good	ok	yes
Ubiquiti Networks Inc	UBNT	49.71	50	3	6.04	good	good	yes

If we want to disclose everything, as per Figure, the most profitable momentum trading stocks are Bitauto (BITA), Himax (HIMX), Ctrip.com (CTRP), Phoenix (FENG), TASER (TASR), Ubiquiti Networks (UBNT) and Methode (MEI).

You should always conduct your own research before you do any sort of investment. This is the smartest thing to do.

Certain fraudulent brokers will try to convince you to invest in underperforming stocks, that may end up in you losing a lot of money. So don't listen to these brokers and please ensure that you do your own research so as to understand the concepts of proper investment. You should aim at earning a high amount of profit through your selections.

Now, from the data given in Fig. 2, you can prepare a strong profitable portfolio so as to get stocks with good option yields:

CTRP BITA HI LCI MX UBNT

Also, you can prepare a separate portfolio that can provide you with similar returns and similar yields. These stocks are:

AER

EJ

CAMP

MEI

TASR

MU

So, if calculations are correct, you have a portfolio with 11 high momentum stocks that give a good yield. These stocks are quite safe, but among all, EJ and AER are quite risky, and are prone to regular price fluctuations.

The remaining stocks are quite low on the risk meter, but it is still not a relief, because risk is always involved with high momentum trading, as opposed to certain stocks that are safe and provide proper dividend amounts.

You could quite easily add XRS to take your portfolio up 12 stocks, but the stock only gives 2.92% yield. But due to the high dividend payment, your total yield will be better.

Step 5: Opening the position

If the direction of the momentum has been properly identified and confirmed accordingly, and after observing an appropriate level of interest on a level 2 screen, the trader can open his stock position. Some momentum traders often choose to wait for the purpose of retesting the support before they make the final decision. But this differs from one trader to the other.

Step 6: Determining the level of exit

When a trader is trading in momentum stocks, he or she will be targeting to make a certain amount of profit within a short time period. These traders are always active in the stock market, even after opening only a single stock position and placing a single order. Their activity is position oriented and the elements that led to the opening of the position.

These traders will always be on the lookout for a particular saturation point of any trade. When he or she opens a long term position, he or she will hold out till the bidding interest decreases and offering interest increases. This may or may not be supported by a drastic decrease in trading volume.

This is perhaps the most common signal that allows a momentum trader to close a position and enjoy the profits.

Chapter 9: A trade going wrong – identifying a situation

Similar to any other variety of stock trading, a momentum trader will also make mistakes in multiple trading sessions. But these traders are quite dynamic in nature. If any trade starts to go down, they will not stick around and wait for the situation to improve. Their well trained and focused approach towards trading allows them to cut their losses accordingly and swiftly.

Any winning or losing stock position cannot be kept for more than one minute, or for the entire day right up to the closing hours of a standard trading day. Usually, any short term momentum trading position is usually closed in the very first hour of the day's trade, traders can try and keep the position open for a bit longer to earn a higher profit from the increased momentum in the latter half of the day.

If any trader holds the stock for so long, it is quite normal that you will not find him in his chair, keeping an eye on a level 2 screen and trading charts. Placing a stop loss order to secure all profits is always a smart idea, so as to allow the trader to look into any other stock.

But no experienced momentum trader will hold a certain stock position for more than one day – he will close right before the trading day is over.

Chapter 10: Reasons why people choose momentum trading

Momentum trading has more downsides than any other form of trading existing in this world. Any momentum trader must analyse potential trades before the market opens, and after the market opens, fully focus on target positions that remain open.

Deciding to buy or sell stocks requires a lot of experience in the fields of interpreting level 2 screens and understanding trading charts, and this also requires a reliable trading system or software that gives fast access to and full functionality of the market. When any trader starts his trade following these protocols, it is quite evident that there will be certain losses at first.

But in case of momentum trading, time spent in front of the screen, analysing charts and what not, can be justified in terms of high yield of profit from any open stock position.

Keep the following question in mind:

Would you earn USD 3.00 on a certain stock, or would you rather make 50 cents?

The very first answer that may pop up in your might be USD 3.00, but if you are momentum trader, and earning USD 3.00 could mean holding on to a stock for a period of 4 months, then it is always better to close on a stock position within one hour and earn 50 cents from it. It will be a much profitable decision.

Momentum trading is also known as and considered to be the best strategy for day treading. Any trader dealing with momentum trading will be able to earn small profiles in a short time period, and that too almost every day. But the trader needs to be experienced to take such risks. Before investing a single dime from the risk capital fund, the trader must spend a lot of time training and understanding the concepts.